STEAL FROM THE PROS

By the same author:

JACKLIN'S GOLF SECRETS (with Tony Jacklin)
THE BOOK OF GOLF DISASTERS
ARNOLD PALMER'S COMPLETE BOOK OF PUTTING
   (with Arnold Palmer)
PREFERRED LIES ABOUT GOLF
The Real Low-down on the Royal and Ancient Game

STEAL FROM THE PROS

To Improve Your Golf

Peter Dobereiner

Illustrations by Albany Wiseman

Stanley Paul
London Melbourne Auckland Johannesburg

For William

Stanley Paul & Co. Ltd

An imprint of Century Hutchinson Ltd

62–65 Chandos Place, London WC2N 4NW

Century Hutchinson Australia (Pty) Ltd
PO Box 496, 16–22 Church Street, Hawthorn, Melbourne, Victoria 3122

Century Hutchinson New Zealand Limited
PO Box 40-086, Glenfield, Auckland 10

Century Hutchinson South Africa (Pty) Ltd
PO Box 337, Bergvlei 2012, South Africa

First published 1988

© The Observer 1988
Illustrations © The Observer 1988

Typeset in Monophoto Ehrhardt by
Vision Typesetting, Manchester

Printed and bound in Great Britain by
Anchor Brendon Ltd, Tiptree, Essex

ISBN 0 09 173697 8

Contents

Introduction

For nearly three years the *Observer* published an intermittent series of golfing hints entitled 'Steal from the Pros'. Albany Wiseman drew the illustrations, working meticulously from photographs to make sure that every detail was correct. As the author I was astonished by the response to this venture. I even had to install a photocopying machine in my home to supply back numbers to readers who were collecting the full set and had missed one or two while on holiday. I had to devote a certain time each week to responding to readers' requests for individual help with golf problems and to sending out reassurances that in the fullness of time the hints would be published in book form. So here it is at last, surely the first book of golf instruction to be produced as a direct result of public demand.

Steal from the Pros is not intended to be a comprehensive teach-yourself-golf primer. The purpose rather was to stimulate golfers to look at fine players with a discriminating eye so that they could recognize the basic virtues of good golf technique and adapt them to their own purposes. As a professional golf watcher I cannot help but observe and overhear spectators discussing the methods of the star players and often I have been dismayed at the confusion of fact with fantasy, cause with consequence. If only, I thought, these spectators were more selective in their observations they would take away truly beneficial images as well as adding to their enjoyment of golf watching.

Then there was the problem of addressing an unseen audience of golfers of every size, shape, gender and standard of attainment. Most written instruction carries with it the implication that if the reader diligently absorbs and practises several hundred different movements and then strings them all together in a smooth sequence, he or she will emerge at the end of the book as a clone of Ben Hogan.

Alas, it is futile to attempt such a process. The brain cannot be programmed like a computer. Quite a simple action, such as transferring a forkload of *canard à l'orange* from plate to mouth, involves more than 10,000 muscular responses and it would be impossible to learn them one by one. Forget number 8,729 and you stick yourself in the ear.

Fortunately the human brain is superior to any computer. It needs only a signal, by sight or sound or both, and it can reproduce an action. But where can we find those signals? The most successful exponents of golf are the obvious sources and for practical purposes that means the tournament professionals.

In fact the tournament pros are not necessarily the best players. The finest putters, for example, are undoubtedly to be found in amateur golf and you will not see the world's longest hitters playing in the Open championship. Greg Norman, reputedly one of the world's most powerful strikers with his drives averaging 280 yards, is a puny hitter compared with the members of the 350 Club. These are players who qualify under strictly controlled conditions by hitting straight drives 350 yards. We need, however, models who are available for analysis, in person or on television, and, after all, most of us would settle for driving 280 yards.

Instead of asking the pros how they hit their shots, we researched the mechanics of the swing and determined how the club-head must behave to produce good shots. Those were not unduly complicated calculations since there are only five conditions which the club-head has to satisfy in order to hit the ball far and straight. Then we isolated the essential elements in golfers' swings that produced these five club-head conditions.

We photographed them, but photographs make poor signals. The eye is not drawn to the essential point; it tends to be distracted by irrelevancies, flitting from the position of the player's head to his grip or his leg action. So we gave the photographs to an artist with the skill to emphasize the vital lesson.

The result is a series of basic images, reinforced by a few explanatory words, which together reproduce the *feel* of the golf swing. A photograph shows you what the swing looks like; this series seeks to tell you how to achieve it.

We concentrate on the fundamentals, making the series suitable for beginners, but since the series is concerned with basics every golfer of any standard should benefit. After all, when Sandy Lyle hits a 240-yard one-iron slightly off line it is because of a fault in one of those basics, just as it is for the duffer who slices wildly into the trees.

Above all, we hope that the series will enable golfers to look at the stars with new eyes, seeing things that they had never noticed before and understanding them. If you know what to look for then surely you will find it.

PART 1

THE PRELIMINARIES

How you hold the club, how you stand and how you set yourself to the ball can be compared to loading, cocking and aiming a gun. Unless these are done right you do not stand a chance of hitting the target when you pull the trigger.

Forget your right arm

The reason we have amputated some of the vital working parts of Graham Marsh is to dramatize the most important, and least understood, factor in golf.

By far the commonest reason for bad shots is that the right hand and arm overpower the swing and ruin it, causing low hooks, high slices and fluffs. Almost every handicap player would improve just by pondering the golden rule before every shot: *Golf is* *a left-handed game for right-handed people.*

The right hand does play a part but its contribution is automatic, without conscious effort, and for an effective swing it should feel as if the right hand is a passive passenger.

The golfer may think that he is denying himself a major source of power by taking his right hand out of the action but in fact he is increasing his potential for both length and control.

Keep left for the right angle

Here is the proof of why golf has to be a left-handed game for right-handed people. With a right-handed swing, which is the same as a two-handed swing in which the right hand has taken control, the axis of the swing becomes the right shoulder. Inevitably, the club-head must be coming from out to in – that is, moving on a line well to the left of the target – when it reaches the ball, and a contortionist could not hit a decent shot with that angle of approach. But shift the axis to the left shoulder and the arc of the swing brings the club-head along an in-to-out path, the essential angle of attack for a good shot.

Getting to grips

Having established that golf is a left-handed game for right-handed people, we can now understand the value of that unnatural and seemingly feeble arrangement, the Vardon grip. One of the main reasons for overlapping the little finger of the right hand, as demonstrated by Nathaniel Crosby, is to reduce right-hand dominance. Likewise the grip of the left hand should be firm, not strangling-the-bank-manager tight but firm, while the grip of the right hand should be relaxed.

By all means interlock that little finger with the first finger of the left hand if you prefer, the method which has served Jack Nicklaus well enough, but at all events think and feel left-handed.

Gently does it

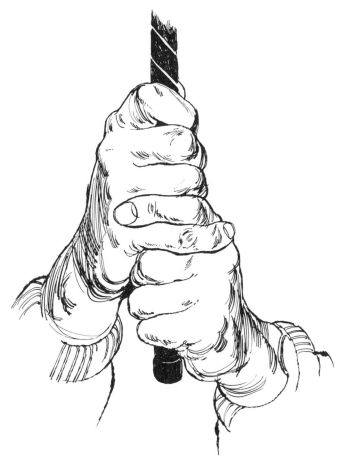

An effective grip is the first prerequisite of good golf but what is effective for Bernhard Langer may not necessarily suit you. If you have given the overlapping, or Vardon, grip a good trial – and it takes time before it feels comfortable and natural – you might experiment with the interlocking grip, as favoured by Jack Nicklaus. Conventionally the overlapping grip is suggested for people with small hands but Sandy Lyle has large hands and he has used it with great success. One advantage of interlocking is that it prevents any tendency for the hands to slip out of position during the swing.

The most important element of the grip is the tension; the grip should be formed on the club so lightly that it is only just possible to swing the club without having it slip through the fingers.

Don't choke yourself

Now here's a curiosity. As he addresses the ball Mark McNulty's right forefinger is not even on the club but pointing at his left foot. Does he play like this? The answer is no; as he takes the club back his finger assumes the normal position around the grip. The reason for this idiosyncratic method is to give him a last-minute reminder not to swing the club with a pincer grip between thumb and forefinger, a natural tendency and one of the many ways to spoil the shot. In everyday life we use those powerful and wonderfully adapted digits for all work requiring strength and precision so the novice is conditioned to apply them to golf. It does not work. A tight grip with the right thumb and forefinger inhibits a free swing and throws the club-head off line. The right hand should rest *lightly* on the club, a virtual passenger, while the left hand directs operations.

But, you may ask, does that method not rob us of a valuable source of power and precision? Not at all. The right hand comes into play through the impact zone, providing extra zip, and there is no need consciously to tighten the grip for this purpose. That happens automatically.

Break the habit

This is not such an uncommon sight as you might imagine, a golfer gripping the club with his left hand below the right. Many children grip a club naturally like this. Quite a few of them never switch to a conventional grip and become accomplished players. You can see several cack-handed golfers in any South African professional tournament and one of them, the late Sewsunker Sewgolum, won several big tournaments, in Europe and Africa. Our model is a Portuguese caddie and he plays a respectable game.

There are certain advantages in this style but on balance they are outweighed by the disadvantages. If your child shows a preference for holding the club like this, then gently but firmly direct him onto the path of orthodoxy. And unless there are powerful reasons against such a move, the same advice holds for a child whose natural inclination is to play left-handed. Do not worry about warping his psyche; right-handed golf should be primarily a left-sided game.

Aim the right way

aiming point

It may sound odd but it is a fact that the part of Severiano Ballesteros's game which the other professionals most admire is the way he sets up to the ball. They appreciate that hitting the target depends on the way you aim the gun and nobody does it better than Seve. It looks easy enough but how many golfers achieve such a natural and relaxed address position? Note that the shoulders, hips and feet are perfectly aligned on the target, that the arms hang down vertically, without tension; that the chin points at the ball rather than being pressed against the chest. He is comfortable, balanced and loose and, since he also has a good grip, he is more than halfway towards making a good shot before he starts his upswing. At this stage 90 per cent of golfers have already ruled out any possibility of hitting the ball well.

Set store by the set-up

The stylish Australian Ian Baker-Finch has an excellent set-up, which is why he hits such superb shots. Note in particular how his left arm and club are virtually one entity, a long lever straight from shoulder to the club-head. The right shoulder is dropped to allow his relaxed right arm to reach a comfortable grip below the left hand, with that right shoulder held well back.

Observe also the ball position, midway between the feet, for this fairway wood shot. The vast majority of golfers, including some professionals, play this shot with the ball opposite the left toe and then wonder why the ball does not get airborne; the loft on the club-head cannot do its essential work properly unless contact is made at the lowest point of the swing.

Sit up straight

Bernard Gallacher is not exceptionally tall at five foot nine so why does he find it necessary to bend his knees to this degree to play an iron shot? Well, this is one of the secrets of his enduring success over a quarter of a century of top-class golf as amateur and pro. The instruction books tell us to stand up tall and proud for golf but, like so many other valuable pieces of advice, that exhortation needs amplification. It is better to think back to the schoolroom instruction to sit up straight. The important point is to keep a straight back, since the spine is well enough adapted to twisting. The complications, in both an orthopaedic and a golfing sense, arise when we twist with a bent spine. Like everyone else, Gallacher has had to withdraw from tournaments on occasion, once because his cat was sick, but never because of back problems. So by all means think tall and proud with the upper body and take in a reef with the knees to set yourself within easy reach of the ball.

The beanpole squat

For tiresome scientific reasons concerning the action of a flail it is impractical to employ golf clubs which are more than an inch or two longer than standard. So golfers who are longer than standard have a problem. Bending down to reach the ball is the natural and worst possible answer and makes the golfer a prime candidate for the osteopath's couch. Everyone knows that lifting heavy weights with a bent spine puts intolerable strain on the spine but we do not associate golf with lifting. In fact at impact on a full shot there is a pull down the shaft equivalent to lifting a sack of potatoes and the strain is compounded by the rotation of the spine.

Tall golfers should model themselves on George Archer, six foot five, who addresses the ball with a weightlifter's stance, knees bent, weight slightly back on the heels and a straight spine. He maintains this squatting posture until he hits the ball but immediately after impact he draws himself up to his full height with a hollow-backed finish.

Ache for success

The occupational disorder of golfers is backache. Our sport practically maintains the profession of osteopathy and most of this lumbar discomfort is caused by faulty technique. If your style of play involves both a bending and a twisting of the spine, you are a prime candidate for back problems.

It would be a gross impertinence to suggest that Don January had a faulty technique but this tall and willowy Texan used to be a martyr to his back and the pain threatened to end his career prematurely. His solution was to adopt an exaggeratedly upright stance, playing even the long irons from a position

barely a foot in front of a line drawn between his toes. From this position he can keep his spine straight as he turns, albeit with a slight loss of length.

You might think that he could achieve the same effect by using clubs with over-length shafts, but longer shafts create problems with centrifugal force and timing. There used to be a vogue for telling pupils that it was impossible to stand too close to the ball at the address, a theory now happily discredited, but if you are getting twinges in the lower back you might find salvation in January's method.

Fuzzy thinking

Who among us would not like to play as well as Fuzzy Zoeller? But who would pay his price of constant pain and back surgery? Here he is playing a short pitch shot but his posture is simply an exaggerated version of his stance for full shots and you do not have to be an orthopaedic surgeon to wince at the strain on his back.

Club-heads weigh less than half a pound for the driver, becoming progressively heavier for the shorter clubs but still less than a pound. Yet in a full swing those weights increase more than a hundredfold and at impact in a full-blooded drive the golfer is resisting a pull down the shaft in the order of 110 pounds. That is the equivalent of two suitcases loaded to the airline limit plus the family ration of duty frees, or one strapping jockey.

An awareness of those statistics may not help you to play better golf but it may persuade you to think about posture and to conclude that since your task as a golfer is approaching that of a weightlifter then you would do well to copy the weightlifter's stance: bottom out, spine straight and head up. Golf is a game for a lifetime but only if you play with a straight back.

Giving bad shots the elbow

It is a popular myth that today's champions play better than their predecessors. The essentials of golf are eternal because they are simply expressions of the unchanging laws of nature and we have selected the 1936 Open champion, Alf Padgham, as the model. While we should always think of the swing as a continuous movement rather than a sequence of classical positions, it is useful to stop the action and check that the vital components are in place. Note Padgham's right elbow. At the address it is tucked *in front* on his right hip and at the top of the upswing it is still as close to his ribcage as it can be commensurate with comfort and easy movement. Controlling any tendency for that right elbow to fly away from the body is one of the keys to good golf.

Small is beautiful

Ian Woosnam is the victim of many unfunny remarks about his lack of height but the Welsh Ryder Cup star positively towers above Miguel Martin of Spain who stands only five foot one. The good news for shorter golfers is that Martin has no trouble competing with the strapping six-footers and, like Woosnam, is an exceptionally efficient striker. Inch for inch and pound for pound the little Spaniard is probably the best player in Europe and he is getting better each year. His action is a model for shorter golfers. If he swung in an upright plane he would have to use shorter clubs and his game would be miniaturized. Instead he uses standard clubs and swings them in a markedly flat plane, which means that he has to position himself well back from the ball. Lay a ruler along the shaft of the club, however, and you will see that it points directly at the ball, meaning that the plane of his swing is perfect. That flat swing gives him the widest possible arc, hence the greatest possible distance. Slugging is not the way to compensate for lack of stature. Here is the answer, combined with rhythm and balance.

PART 2

THE SWING

In the final analysis all that matters is that half of a thousandth of a second when the club-head is in contact with the ball and the purpose of the swing is to maximize your potential for the vital moment.

Pointers to set you on the right lines

aiming point

swing down on this line...

to hit on this line...

The business part of the swing is initiated by turning the hips back until the belt buckle is facing the ball again, the point which Gary Cullen has reached in this picture. The left heel, raised to accommodate the backswing, returns firmly to earth and only now does the left arm really start its accelerating downward pull. The danger is for the powerful right arm to try to get into the act at this point, throwing the right shoulder forwards and deflecting the club-head from its swing path.

For beginners it is a sound plan to lay a club on the turf as shown here, pointing about ten degrees right of the target, and swing the club along that line. Don't worry; the ball will go straight. The golfer is the victim of an optical illusion because his eyes are well ahead of the plane of the swing, so when he aims to swing to the right of the target he actually swings on line.

Unreliable evidence of the eyes

People get most dreadfully confused when they are told not to swing along the target line but to swing from in to out, that is to say as if aiming right of the target. Why? Well, it is all because of an optical illusion. The club-head is swung in a more or less inclined plane and if our eyes were set in line with that plane, about in the centre of the chest, then the club-head would be seen to travel along the target line, as shown in the first drawing. But our heads in fact pierce that plane and we are looking down on the arc, hence the impression that we are swinging at the ball from the wrong angle. And that is the impression that we must have.

If that all sounds too complicated then take it on trust and use the well-tried image much beloved of the late Dai Rees. Imagine a clock face superimposed on the ball and swing through from four to ten.

Maintain the triangle

It is impossible to overemphasize the importance of turning the shoulders during the swing. It is not quite true that the arms play no part in hitting the ball beyond connecting the club to the body but that is not a bad thought for beginners to keep in mind. It prevents golf's deadly sin of holding the body static and swinging the arms across the chest. Notice here how Bobby Cole has taken the club back as far as the waist-high position and his arms are still in the same position relative to his shoulders as they were at the address. That whole triangle of arms

and shoulders has not changed shape at all and the backswing is being effected solely by shoulder turn.

There are a couple of tricks to help you from picking up the club with the hands and arms. At the address apply light pressure with the right hand, using the right arm as a brace to maintain the geometry of that triangle. Alternatively, you can indoctrinate yourself by repeating the swing thought of the day: Never let your left arm obscure your left nipple. Swing with the shoulders and let the arms go hang.

Rock 'n' roll golf

There is only one Lee Trevino and that is the way it should remain. However, Trevino's individual style does illustrate two fundamentals of golf which are well worth stealing and adapting. Note the direction from which the club-head is approaching the ball; it looks as if he is hitting a cover drive well right of the target. At this point he is rolling his hands to bring the club-face square to the shot, with his right elbow almost touching his hip. But the main observation to be made is how his hips have turned, with belt buckle pointing at his target, before he makes contact with the ball.

Instructors talk of clearing the hips but, if that expression conveys the impression of merely getting them out of the way to give the arms room to swing freely, it is misleading. Trevino's hip turn is part of a powerful rotation of the torso, using the big muscles of the back like a javelin thrower, to accelerate the club-head.

The hip turn is not a passive preparation for the swing; it is the essence of the swing itself.

Start down with the hips

We have seen how golfers use the powerful muscles of the back and thighs to accelerate the club-head by rotating the torso. Here we see the beginning of the process as Nick Faldo starts the downswing.

Forget any talk you may have heard about the backswing being like coiling a spring, with the suggestion of elastic being stretched to the limit. Muscles are not elastic. The backswing should be slow and relaxed and the rotation should be from top to bottom: starting with the hands, followed by the shoulders and then the hips.

This order is reversed for the downswing. The rotation is initiated by the hips as you can see here, with the hips having returned to the square position while the hands have barely moved. That progression continues with mounting power, the hips leading the shoulders and the shoulders leading the hands in an accelerating rotation. Imagine hurling a javelin from a stationary position and the muscular progression of the swing will become clear. Of course, for golf the javelin must be thrown downwards rather than up but otherwise the power build-up is similar.

Straight arm tactics

Sam Torrance is one of the strongest and most stylish players in the world and this left-arm position as he starts his downswing is the key to his success. He has made a full turn of the shoulders and now, as he shifts his weight onto the left leg, his extended left arm is pulling along the line of the shaft. That left elbow will not bend in a chopping action but will lock out, giving him the widest possible arc and the maximum club-head speed at impact.

If your left elbow is bent at this point, which is the natural way to unleash the awesome strength of your powerful right arm, then you do not have a chance of making a good shot.

The invisible pivot

Golfers often speak of the pivot but what is the difference between a pivot and a body turn? Well, you can make a full body turn while your head is swaying all over the place; a pivot implies rotation around a fixed spindle, like a hinge. Here T. C. Chen gives a fine demonstration of the pivot principle. Although his body sways and arches as he transfers his weight to the left side, his feet and head are firmly anchored, merely rotating on that vital but invisible pivot.

By all means slide the hips to the left as you plant the full weight onto the left foot but just make sure that your head does not slide too. It may help to remember the advice of that wisest of golfers, Bobby Jones, who said that he liked to feel he was looking underneath the ball as he hit it. At impact the body mass should be ahead of the ball, the head held firmly behind it.

Make the right turn

aiming point

The backswing is not just a lifting of the club with the hands. That's fine for beating carpets but useless for golf. The backswing is effected by a turning of the entire body as far as it will go against a braced right leg, until the shoulders have rotated through ninety degrees. Bill Longmuir's position is perfect with his chin brushing his left shoulder,

left arm straight and his club pointing like a gun barrel straight at his target.

Try taking the club back, holding the pose and asking a friend to check your form. From Longmuir's position golf is a game of routine; from any other arrangement golf is a frustrating exercise in hit or miss.

Stay loyal to your friends

Modern golf really started with this man, six times Open champion Harry Vardon. See how his wrists have rolled through the shot, a rather exaggerated finish by today's standards but that action had to be emphasized with hickory shafts. Vardon's reinvention of the golf swing began with a reappraisal of the implements of the game and his attention to this aspect of golf is well worth stealing.

He had clubs built which were light enough for him to control during every inch of the swing and that should be the first consideration in selecting clubs. Thereafter there is not much that can go wrong with clubs and they can last a lifetime. But it is worthwhile to have them professionally checked once a year. When you have had a set for some time you have an investment in them, in having your muscles attuned to their weight and balance, so do not discard them lightly. Have the lofts and lies of the irons checked, the woods refinished and new grips all round every winter. That way you get the psychological uplift from their gleaming appearance plus the advantages of playing with trusty old friends.

Delay that hit

The late hit, exemplified here in this study of Peter Oosterhuis, is the holy grail of golf. Everyone searches for it and nobody finds it for the simple reason that it does not exist. It is a myth and the sooner the phrase is eliminated from the vocabulary of golf the better. What there is, however, and it is one of the prime causes of duff shots, is the early hit, or hitting from the top. The player gets to the top of his swing and then immediately lunges with all the power he can exert and that convulsive effort is dissipated by the time the club-head reaches the ball.

The answer is to start the downswing *slowly* and it may help deliberately to hold that angle between arms and club at the start of the downswing. Now, as you accelerate the downswing, centrifugal force opens that angle (provided that you keep those shoulders rotating) and at impact the club is in line with the left arm, not early, not late, but perfectly timed. So start down slowly and save that surge of power for the hitting zone, when your hands are approaching waist height.

How to tame the tyrant

Of course you do not hit the ball with the follow-through but how you finish the shot can tell you a lot about why it was a good shot, or a bad one. If you hit a real purler, as Mark James has just done, then the impetus of the swing will leave you pretty much in this position, with your weight mainly supported on the outside of the left foot, belt buckle facing the target, hands high and perfectly in balance. Unless a full shot leaves you in this position you are almost certainly allowing that tyrant, the right arm, to dominate your swing.

Spin those shoulders

A major distinction between long-handicap golfers and the accomplished strikers is that the rabbit tends to hit *at* the ball while the tiger swings *through* the ball. For the professional the ball is an incidental mark on the path of his accelerating swing.

That is easily said but how is it done? Do you spin the hips in a pirouette? Or flash through the impact zone with the hands? Well, these things happen in some degree but the main thing, the genuine

secret of long hitting, the action on which the golfer should concentrate his attention, is to rotate the *shoulders* through the shot. Try imagining that you are sweeping the ball away with that right shoulder in the manner demonstrated here by Sam Torrance. Just as the shoulders initiate the upswing so they finish the downswing with a surge of power through impact. If the shoulders quit their rotation at impact, the shot is both feeble and uncontrolled.

Question of balance

Golfing truths are eternal and one of them is here illustrated by the immortal Walter Hagen. He was never the greatest of stylists, being better known as a brilliant improvizer, but the one constant factor in the play of this great champion was that he maintained a perfect balance on every shot. At the completion of this shot he was like a rock.

If you find that you have a tendency to wobble, sway, or even topple forwards at the top of the follow-through, the odds are that you had the ball out of position at the address. Check by regaining your equilibrium and then, without adjusting your feet, make a languid practice swing. If your club-head brushes the turf anywhere except on the divot scrape of your previous shot, there you have the solution to your problem. If, however, your practice swing contacts the ground precisely on the spot of your real shot, then the probability is that the fault lies in over-hitting.

Don't look now

Ronan Rafferty, one of the brightest prospects of European golf, clips one away and there are two tips we can steal from his action. Note first how his hands are rolling, right over left, on the follow-through, continuing the process which started on his downswing in order to square the club-face at impact. Notice also that he is still looking at the ball position, even though the ball itself is a hundred yards away by now.

Premature looking up to follow the flight of the shot is the ruination of golf. Have faith. Resist the impulse to see the result of the shot too soon. If you do not try to watch where the ball is going it is more likely to find its own way straight up the fairway. If you are too eager to watch its progress every inch of the way, you are liable to watch it head into the trees on a sickeningly low trajectory and probably bouncing as it disappears.

The girls have a secret – speed

Are you secretly troubled and perplexed by the thought, powerfully muscled and finely honed athlete that you are, that you do not hit the ball far enough? Do you wonder whether the slip of a girl who drives the ball 20, 30, 50, 100 yards farther than you is employing some secret move which the books and instructors have kept from you? And do you resolve to give the ball an even dirtier great smash next time? If so, welcome to the club. This power fixation results in a tendency to plant the feet like a weightlifter, to grasp the club as if it were a two-handed broadsword and to concentrate your effort in those mighty arm muscles. This emphasis on physical strength guarantees a disappointing shot and you are lucky if you even make a clean contact with the ball.

Try changing your ambition. Instead of hitting the ball hard, think about club-head speed. The aim should be to accelerate the club-head gradually to make the shaft sing as it cuts through the air and the club-head to whoosh at 1000 miles an hour through the strike zone. By switching your intention from power to speed your body will react automatically, with a loose, free swing. That's how those women get the distance.

Legs are for walking

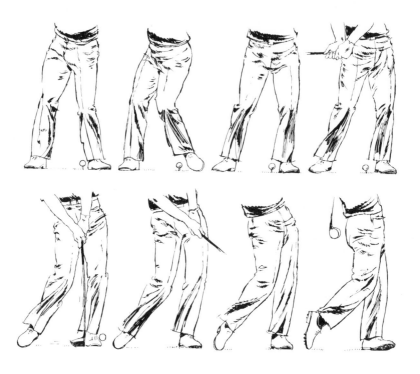

Golfers who wish to improve, even tournament players, often speak about improving their leg action. They should watch one of Severiano Ballesteros's clinics and see how he hits a drive 260 yards while standing on one leg. The legs do not contribute to a good swing; leg action is a *reaction* to a good swing, following as naturally as night follows day if the club-head is swung through the correct arc. The same goes for shifting the weight, leg-drive through the ball and all the other mythology below the waist. Concentrate on swinging the club-head properly and the legs will look after themselves.

Exorcise the shank

There is one uneven lie situation which can be fraught with some danger, namely the position in which Henry Cotton found himself here with the ball well below the level of his feet. This is the classical condition for the unspeakable horror of the shank, in which the ball is struck with the hosel of the club and squirts off at an eccentric angle. The ultimate crisis occurs when one shank breeds another, and another, from any lie and with every short pitch shot, and the golfer develops a full-blown neurosis.

Fortunately the precaution is also the cure and the first rule, as with all nervy shots, is to grip the club *lightly*. Favour the weight back on the heels. Swing back slowly and as fully as is commensurate with the length of the shot; it is a dangerous fallacy to assume that a short backswing and a jab at the ball will deliver the club-face more accurately to the target. Trust the weight of the club-head to do the work and follow through at least as far as the downswing, at the same tempo as for a full shot.

Some teachers reckon that it is impossible to hit a shank deliberately. Do not risk it, for no good can come from fooling about with the dark and evil forces of the devilish shank.

Countering the bad lie

Most instruction books go into complicated detail about how to play from uneven lies, with diagrams showing where to put your feet for uphill, downhill and sidehill shots plus a mass of heavy advice about taking care not to hook or slice. Even if the poor golfer could remember all these drills, his or her mind would be buzzing with so much geometric theory that the shot would almost certainly go wrong.

Golf should be a simple and natural game and fortunately there is a simple and natural solution to the problem of uneven lies. Your body knows very well how to stand on a slope, so let your instincts work out the complexities of weight distribution and equilibrium. Stand away from the ball on a similar slope and make a practice swing. Notice where the club-head brushes the turf and you have all the information you need about ball position. Stand to the ball accordingly and let rip, as demonstrated here by the late Alf Padgham.

PART 3

THE
SHORT GAME

Golf can never be a game of perfection,
only a striving towards perfection.
Chipping, pitching, sand play and putting
are the areas of golf where we can heal our
self-inflicted wounds and emerge without
damage to our scores.

Hitting the right pitch

The short pitch shot causes problems for handicap players, especially when it must be played over an obstacle such as a bunker. Because it is a gentle shot, and a nervy one, club golfers tend to restrict the backswing and tighten their hands on the grip, causing a convulsive jab which all too often scuffles the ball into the sand.

Watch David Llewellyn's style. He makes a long backswing, with that left arm dominating the club every inch of the way, and then at the same leisurely tempo he makes an accelerating attack at the ball, a firm and positive stroke which pops the ball high into the air. He thus gets plenty of backspin on the ball and this enables him to toss it right up to the flag.

Hitting the right tempo

Brian Marchbank is hitting 50-yard pitch shots over a bunker to the flag. This is the situation which produces maximum anxiety among club golfers, generating tension and resulting in an ugly lunge at the ball, with the head coming up prematurely to observe the fate of the shot. All too often that fate is precisely the one which the golfer was most concerned to avoid: a half-topped scuffle into the sand.

Marchbank demonstrates the vital ingredient for success: almost a full backswing. He plays the shot almost in slow motion with a leisurely upswing and starting back at the same lazy tempo so that he can accelerate the club-head through the ball with a positive, attacking contact which pops the ball high into the air with maximum backspin.

Practise for keeps

What are Glenn Ralph and Peter Barber doing? Chipping, obviously, and they are devoting an entire afternoon to their practice. But unlike club golfers, whose practice sessions are mainly aimless and useless exercises in grooving faults, these professionals are practising with a purpose. They are chipping four balls apiece to a distant hole and then putting out, and matching their aggregate scores for money. Not much money, it is true, but enough to create competitive tension. Anybody can chip a putt well when it does not matter, so they introduce a gambling element to make it matter. Even if the prize is just a beer in the clubhouse it helps to have an incentive because pressure shots are the ones you will need to play on the course.

Note how Ralph favours his weight on the left foot for this shot.

Minimize the risks

There are some techniques which the average golfer is well advised not to steal from the pros. The most obvious shot to avoid is the professional method of chipping from off the green with a sand iron, which Gordon Brand jr is playing here. They lay the blade open and skid the club-head under the ball, imparting maximum backspin. That is fine for them but, unless you play every day and have an exceptional touch, this shot carries too high a risk for general use.

Unless there is an intervening obstruction, the safe and equally effective method is to take a mid-iron and play it like an approach putt. The aim should be to carry the ball through the air to land on the nearest point of the green so that it settles into a roll as soon as possible. Indeed, your first thought with such shots should be to use your putter from off the green.

If the grass is too shaggy, consider a mid-iron as your second option. Only if conditions absolutely demand a lofted trajectory should you reach for a wedge, the club of last resort.

Putt with an iron

Manuel Pinero is noted for his exceptional short game and he owes his successful career to the ability to tidy up from around the green. No matter how well a golfer hits his long approach shots he is always at the mercy of gusting winds and a vital ingredient in the tournament professional's repertory is the skill to save par by getting up and down in two strokes. Mastery of these touch shots probably represents the biggest gulf between the good amateur and the pro, and the tournament specialists spend many hours a week practising pitches and chips. By comparison they find sand play so easy that practice is confined to a few shots to familiarize themselves with

the texture of the sand at each tournament course.

Watching Pinero playing from the fringe the casual observer may be perplexed by his choice of club, sometimes the wedge but often the seven-iron from what appears to be a similar situation. His rule is that if he has to carry the ball over a considerable distance of fringe, say 10 yards or so, and check the shot with backspin, he uses the wedge. But if he is closer to the green and has plenty of putting surface to allow the ball to roll up to the flag, he uses the seven-iron. This is the much safer shot for the weekend golfer, he insists, and the safest way to play it is exactly like a long approach putt.

Chip off the old block

This old timer seems thoroughly confused. He is playing a chip shot yet he is holding the club with a reverse overlap grip, a method which we enlightened modern players know to be reserved exclusively for putting.

But wait a minute. What is a chip shot? It is simply an approach putt played with a lofted club. So if you have a special grip which gives you maximum feel and control of the putter, would it not make sense to

employ that same grip for a chip? Well, this chap did. In 1945 he won nineteen tournaments, eleven of them in succession, and had a stroke average of 68.33. This study of Byron Nelson was drawn from a photograph taken when one of the greatest players of all time was at his prime. If it suited Nelson's purposes to see the chip shot as a putt played with a different club then it might very well be a good idea for us to follow his example.

Right way to get out of a trap

There are several different techniques for playing from sand, depending on the circumstances, and we might as well begin with the standard splash shot from a greenside bunker, as here demonstrated by Bernard Gallacher.

Notice first that he has set up as if to play a shot well to the left of the target, i.e. an exaggerated open stance. The second vital point, detailed in the insert, is that his club face is laid wide open, that is with the face almost horizontal. He takes a *full*, rather steep backswing which brings the club-head down on a steeper angle of attack than normal, accelerating the club-head down into the sand about two inches behind the ball. The objective should be to skim the club-head under the ball without touching it and without any tendency to scoop the ball out of the sand. The club-face will do that as the rounded flange on the back of the club forces the club-head to pull out of its dive. Although the club is swung along a line left of target, the opening of the club-face tends to send the ball to the right of the target. The mean result of these opposing forces is that the ball pops out high from the sand straight towards the flag.

This is one shot in which there must be no rolling of the wrists through the impact zone. Hold that club-face open right through to a high follow-through.

Sand in the works

Ball comes out high along this line...

club swung along this line, well left of target

Target line

It is a matter of common observation that most golfers step into bunkers in a state of suppressed hysteria, dreading the coming ordeal and just hoping to get the thing out of the sand. They are tense, jab violently behind the ball and as often as not leave it in the bunker. All this arises from the fact that they never get themselves into a position from which it is possible to play an effective explosion shot.

Note the salient points of Peter Teravainen's set-up: ball opposite the right toe, left foot well withdrawn from the target line in an open stance, hands ahead of the ball, and the blade of the club laid wide open, almost flat, head over the ball. From here the club is picked up steeply in a full and relaxed upswing and then accelerated into the sand about two inches behind the ball with a descending blow swung along a line connecting the toes, i.e. cutting across the target line.

In normal golfing terms these instructions are all 'faults' but in combination they add up to the classical splash shot. Do not scoop, the flange on the club will deflect the club-head out of the sand, throwing the ball and a cushion of sand towards the flag on a high trajectory. Easy. And one of the most satisfying shots in golf as you get the hang of it.

Real golfers don't cry

One of the commonest sounds on a golf course is the groan, of which there are two distinct types: the high-pitched expression of anguish as the ball heads for trouble, and the groan of despair in a lower register when the player sees the lie of his ball. That first groan of disappointment at your own performance is perhaps permissible, but the second type of groan is unacceptable. The golfer must approach every shot with a sense of eager anticipation, rejoicing when an unusual lie gives him an opportunity to employ his exceptional talents.

Wet or hard-packed sand is a frequent provocation for the despairing groan but, honestly, such a lie offers greater scope than your favourite dry and fluffy sand for a satisfactory result. All it needs is a minor adjustment in technique and, if you are a groaner, a major adjustment in attitude. First, assess whether your putter will do the job. If not, set yourself for a normal explosion shot but think in terms of a wristy skimming shot with the open face of your wedge entering the sand no more than an inch behind the ball rather than the regular two inches. Do not roll the wrists but hold the blade open through the shot and the ball will pop out with lots of lovely backspin.

Anything goes – if it goes in

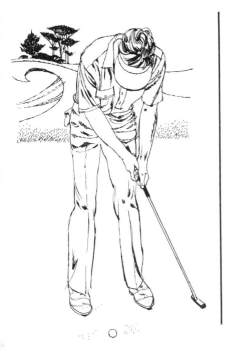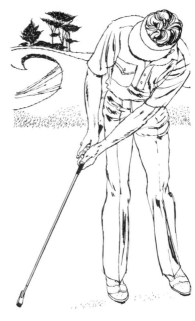

Putting is an individual activity and anything goes so long as it works. But what if it does not work? Well, what many professionals do is study the action of a good putter and copy it. And nobody is the subject of this sincerest form of flattery more than Bob Charles because nobody putts better than he does. He supports the putter with his right hand (right-handers must transpose these instructions, naturally) and keeps that wrist inflexible. The left hand takes the putter back and then pushes it through, about the same distance in each direction. This putt was a 30-footer. The technique is easy enough and, according to Charles, does not have much to do with holing putts. The important thing, he says, is to believe with an unshakable faith that the ball is going to plop dead into the centre of the hole. Alas, we cannot steal faith.

Low can be the key

How far in front of your nose do you hold the work when you thread a needle? The distance varies among individuals according to the state of their eyesight. For delicate work we instinctively adopt a position which brings the object into sharpest focus, and putting is delicate work. Andy North, an exceptionally tall man, grips well down his putter, effectively halving the length of the shaft, because by doing so his eyes are in position for his optimum focal length. (He also gets the bonus of having the butt of the club pressed against the inside of his left forearm,

preventing a collapse of his wrist.)

In settling on a putting method the first consideration should be to adopt a comfortable posture which gives you the sharpest image of the ball. How low can you get? Well, Joe Turness once won the Metropolitan Open putting one-handed with a club the size of a tack hammer. Some golfers are inhibited and defy their instincts for fear of looking silly. There is nothing silly about a method which delivers the goods so, if you feel like it, get down to the job of putting.

Off the target

Ten minutes to go before tee-off time so, being properly concerned to do yourself justice, you go for some practice putting. Your motives are excellent but this can be one way of sapping your confidence and ensuring a bad score. Suppose your practice putts are woefully inadequate. What frame of mind will you take onto the course?

A better preparation is to putt without targets. Concentrate on making a smooth, accelerating stroke, connecting with the sweet spot of the blade every time, and noticing how far the ball rolls. Hit level putts,

downhill putts and uphill putts, paying particular attention to the roll of the ball. That way you will get a feel for the pace of the greens, which is the factor that varies from day to day, and your confidence will not be impaired.

At some clubs the texture of the practice putting green is quite different to that of the greens on the course, in which case a session of practice before a round is a positive hindrance. Agitate within your own club to guarantee that the practice green reproduces the precise conditions on the course.

Toe the line

One mark of a good player is that he takes great care to set himself to the shot exactly the same way every time. Many have set routines to ensure precisely the same relationship between the feet and the ball position and if they are interrupted during this countdown procedure they step away and start afresh from the beginning. We would all do well to be equally meticulous in addressing the ball because this is the aiming procedure and if that is inconsistent the shots will be, too.

One exception to this routine is the putting stance. A player may have his feet almost together for one putt and wide apart for another.

There is method in this discrepancy. The relationship between the left foot and the ball is consistent but the position of the right foot changes according to the length of the putt, the right toe acting as a marker to regulate the length of backswing. That system may or may not work for you but it could help if you are continuously short with your putts. The remedy is to shorten the backswing and increase the follow-through and you can use your right toe as a reminder that the club-head must not go back beyond that line, as demonstrated here by Rodger Davis.

Focus on a sweet spot

The human question mark portrayed here is Ken Brown, acknowledged and envied and statistically ratified as one of the deadliest putters in professional golf. We cannot pick up too many hints from watching a great putter because we are all different and what works for him may be quite unsuitable for you. However, that stooped posture is interesting. Another fabulous putter, the amateur Bonallack, bent even lower over the ball.

The reason, I feel sure, is that the nervous responses for precise and delicate work are primarily directed by eyesight as we observe by the way some people thread a needle almost touching their noses and others perform this task at arm's length. We all have a point at which the object of close attention appears in sharpest focus and that includes putting. Sharp focus, clearly enough, is vital if the sweet spot of the putter face is to contact the ball absolutely spot on. So the first factor to be established in choosing a putting style, and length of putter, is your optimum length of focus. That will govern your stance and, to a high degree, your technique.

Saved – by the big toe

Faith can move mountains and what is a slick downhill putt but the side of a mountain? This week's tip is a favourite from the professionals' bag of tricks for saving a stroke. When playing to steeply contoured greens the tournament specialist always aims to leave his ball below the hole because it is easier to control the putter on a firm, uphill putt.

Good intentions do not always result in good consequences, however, and when the ball finishes above the hole on a fast green you are left with an excruciatingly difficult problem of just how gently to play the putt. You know that if you strike the putt too hard the ball will race way past the hole, possibly leaving you two more putts. More often than not, recalling expressions like just brushing the ball with a butterfly's wing, you overcompensate and baby the putt, leaving yourself another downhiller. Have faith and you can eliminate the slope, turning it into a level putt. Strike the ball with the *toe* of the putter, using the stroke for a similar putt on a flat green.

You have to practise this one, like every other tip, preferably on the practice green before you play. Once you have acquired the feel, you eliminate downhill putts and can play those nervous sliders with your usual firm stroke.

One-handed touch

Denis Durnian's routine on the practice putting green is unconventional but, to judge by results, there is merit in it. He starts by putting one-handed, using the right hand only. (Note the over-forties forefinger extended down the shaft, a popular style to improve directional control.) The reason Durnian practises like this is to sharpen his touch.

The natural functions of the hands are for the left hand to steady the work while the right hand performs tasks requiring accuracy – left hand holding the paper still while the right hand does the writing, left hand holding the orange while the right does the peeling, and so on. The same arrangement goes for putting, with the left hand holding the club and the right guiding it. Durnian is simply isolating the business function of putting and concentrating his attention on it.

A splint for the wrist

A common problem which afflicts golfers is that when putting the left wrist flexes involuntarily just before impact, causing the ball to be dragged to the left of the hole. Johnny Miller became a victim to this spasm and his solution was to have an exceptionally long shaft fitted to his putter, 48 inches long.

By tucking the end of this shaft into his armpit the club effectively acts as a splint for his left forearm and that wrist cannot break during the stroke. It is an unconventional solution to an old problem but in golf, and particularly in putting, there is only one test of technique: Does it work?

Putter, heal thyself

Arnold Palmer has accumulated some 3000 putters, many of them sent to him by well-intentioned inventors and designers. No aspect of golf has inspired more research, ingenuity and frivolity than the search for the perfect putter and our illustration shows some of the wilder ideas which Palmer has received.

There is, however, a basic fallacy which frustrates this frenzy of putter designing: in putting it is the singer, not the song. You can putt with any putter. So when you have found a putter which feels right and looks right, stick with it. Every putt you hit represents an investment of feel and experience in the club, treasure not lightly to be discarded. So if your putting goes off, resist the thought of switching clubs. Your club has not changed, therefore it is you who must have gone off. Heal thyself and remain loyal to your true love. The only thing that can go wrong with a putter is the fickle human attachment.

PART 4

PRACTICE

The practice ground is where the golfer thinks about *how* to hit a shot, whereas on the course the golfer must think only about *where* to hit the shot. The practice ground is the best place to steal from the pros, and the best place to absorb what you have stolen.

Practise with purpose

The practice ground is the place to learn golf and experiment; the golf course is the place for thinking about strategy, not technique. Simply beating balls does more harm than good because aimless hitting encourages over-hitting and all you are doing is perfecting a fault. Every shot must be hit with a purpose and to a target and with full concentration. The practice ground is the one place where the golfer can use artificial aids and here Jeff Hawkes lines up with his toes against the shaft of a club, thereby guaranteeing that his alignment is correct.

Never hit a practice shot at full bore but throttle back to a level of effort which enables you to control the club-head throughout the swing. Don't rush the shots. Pause and observe the flight of the ball, noting where it pitches and how it reacts after landing. Absorb that information and allow it to program itself into your subconscious where your instincts can make corrective adjustments if necessary. Vary your shots, hitting one high one and then a low one, or trying fades and draws. If you hit a wild one do not make extreme adjustments but try again with a more leisurely tempo.

The idea is not to teach yourself like a drill sergeant giving instruction on how to slope arms but to maintain a neutral frame of mind which allows you to learn naturally.

The essence of swing

Ernest Jones was, and remains through his writings, the high priest of pure swing. He was a stylish and accomplished professional until he lost a leg on the western front during the First World War and then he emigrated to America and devoted himself to teaching. His message was that you cannot hit with the club-head faster than you can swing it and that attempts to introduce leverage with a surge of muscle power were counterproductive. The best proof of his doctrine was supplied by one of his pupils, Babe Zabarias, who hit the ball farther than any woman before or since.

Jones demonstrated the theory of pure swing by tying his pocket knife onto his handkerchief and swinging it, a simple action which we can all perform naturally, without instruction. That's easy, said his pupils, but what has it got to do with golf? That is golf, said Jones; golf is an easy game. To prove his point, Jones then swung a club and his knife at the same time, showing that if the club and the knife swing in perfect unison, as illustrated here, then the shot is perfect.

This is the finest winter exercise for the housebound golfer because it imparts the very essence of golf: rhythm and timing.

Dig for victory

Here we have a familiar scene, a tournament professional toiling away on the practice ground. Note in particular how Graham Marsh has created a divot scrape which resembles an open-cast mine, an excavation the size of a tea tray. His routine is to position the ball near the back lip of the scrape and to take out a sliver of turf with about half a dozen shots and then to start another row, extending the strip backwards.

This is not desecration. (I knew one club which stopped a pro from using its practice ground because he was taking lumps out of its precious turf!) This system of practising is the method of a considerate professional because a large area of bare earth like this is much easier to restore than a hundred separate divots. There is a further advantage in that by deliberately creating such a neat, denuded area you automatically punch the club-head down and through the ball. Since your purpose is deliberately to take out a clean divot you guarantee the essence of an iron shot, which is to contact the bottom of the ball with a descending blow.

Timing the power surge

How can we reconcile the doctrine of a dominant left side with Tommy Armour's advice to knock the hell out of the ball with the right hand? The answer lies in the word 'timing' and here Lee Trevino illustrates an exercise designed to keep the right hand out of the act until the correct moment for it to make its contribution. Grip a cap, or a similar object, between the upper right arm and the body and hit a shot. The ball must be well on its way before the cap hits the ground. If the right-arm power is applied too early the cap will fall prematurely, but if that right elbow is kept tucked in, and pointing at the ball on the downswing, the right hand can lash the club-head into the ball as hard as you like.

Don't get too slap happy

That splendid piece of American cracker-barrel philosophy, 'If it ain't broke, don't fix it,' is particularly pertinent to golfers, many of whom tinker with their swings even when they are playing well. If you habitually hit the ball straight then do not even read what follows. Leave well alone, without allowing a dangerous thought to come into your mind. But if you spray your shots indiscriminately right or left then help is at hand.

Consider: when you slap someone's face you do not inadvertently land a karate chop with the side of the hand; without any thought or volition on your part you meet the target flush with the palm every time. The club-face is aligned perfectly with the palm of the right

hand, always assuming that your grip is correct, so when you swing, focus your attention on one key thought: you are going to slap the ball with the palm (or its extension, if you like) of the right hand. If the palm of the hand is square to the line of your shot then the club-face must meet the ball square to the line of the shot.

Warning: reserve this image for the latter stage of the downswing. If you become totally slap-happy you may develop a tendency to pick up the club with the hands and lash at the ball. Your swing must still be governed by shoulder rotation, with virtually passive arms, and the slap should be held back until it is time to deliver the club-head flush to the ball.

Lay off for wind

Everyone knows, or very soon discovers from hard experience, that it is a mistake to try to fight a head wind by hitting the ball harder. The only way is to take more club and swing easily. Accomplished players prefer a head wind because they have absorbed the lesson of hitting the ball well rather than hard and the wind helps control of the shot because the ball sits down where it pitches.

The following wind, the treacherous friend so beloved of indifferent players, is the tricky one. How can the player control the destiny of a downwind shot? Part of the answer is to understand that backspin, the factor which makes a ball fly high, will not bite so well down the wind and the trajectory will be lower than normal. So, as John Bland demonstrates in our illustration, the technique is to take less club than normal and to hit the ball higher than usual, paradoxically by hitting down on it, and harder than usual.

For cross-winds the best policy is to take plenty of club and aim off, trusting that the wind will blow your ball back onto your target. Trying to cancel the effect of cross-winds by deliberately fading or drawing the shot is advanced stuff and strictly for the experts.

Read your divots

One mark of a good player is literally a mark, the blemish he leaves on the turf after impact. With a fairway wood, as here played by Roger Fidler, the sole of the club brushes the turf, leaving a long, narrow bruise because his wide swing brings the club-head into the ball on a shallow arc. With irons, the angle of attack is steeper because of the shorter shafts, and the descending club-head contacts first the ball and then the ground, removing a divot of turf. These divots should be long and slim, leaving a scar which points directly at the target. If your fairway woods dent the ground, or if your iron shots gouge out short, stubby divots, it means that you are chopping down on the ball and losing distance. The remedy is to widen your arc and you do this by keeping the club-head low to the ground as you take it back from the ball with a straight left arm.

More power from less effort

Anyone who has played golf for some time will be familiar with the experience of meeting a new opponent, observing his fluent practice swing and thinking: 'I'll have my work cut out today; this chap is a real player.' Then the opponent steps up to his ball and hits it with a completely different, and inferior, action. Phew! What a relief.

Nearly all golfers would cut their scores dramatically if they played their golf with their practice swings. The change from smooth practice swing to muscle-bound lunge is caused by the evil influence of the ball, of course, and the need to belt the daylights out of it. Tension and pressure are the insidious enemies

but they can be defeated. Get them out of your system with your practice swing. Grasp the club with a firm, he-man grip, wind up and rip the club-head through the daisy with every ounce of energy you can summon. Tell yourself: 'Boy! That was a 400-yard blue-flamer. But I only want 300 yards at most out of my shot. So I must relax, just make a smooth swing and cosy the ball up the fairway with three-quarters power.' It may be kidology but it is not a bad deal to get a better result by employing less effort.

Our illustration shows Hugh Jackson loosening up with a couple of violent practice swings to exorcise his tension before settling down to a session of smooth shots.

Cracking the whip

Here we have the five times Open champion Peter Thomson in the first stage of the downswing, illustrating the sequence of the gradual acceleration of the club-head. The backswing rotation starts at the top, initiated by a turning of the shoulders and with the hip turn following in its own good time. But that sequence is reversed for the downswing. Notice how Thomson's hips have returned to the square position while the shoulders have hardly begun to move.

One of the commonest sins of golf is to get the downswing sequence wrong. The player gets to the top and his next movement is a violent lurch of the shoulders and arms, known as hitting from the top. By the time the club-head reaches the ball most of that premature surge of energy has been dissipated and the player cannot understand why such a lusty swipe has produced such a feeble result. The trick is to start the downswing from the bottom and hold back that release of effort for a whip-lash through the ball.

The feel of a champion

Bobby Jones, who hit the ball as well as anyone in the history of the game and who understood the technicalities better than most, also had the gift of conveying the feel of golf. With the driver he said that he felt that he was trying to look at the underside of the ball. Such images can be dangerous because if they are taken too literally you can get yourself into absurd contortions. But if we interpret them sensibly, one mental picture can do the work of hours of instruction. After all, what greater gift could a golfer receive than the opportunity to inhabit Bobby Jones' body as he unleashes a full-blooded drive?

This study of Christy O'Connor may help to illuminate Jones's feeling of trying to look at the underside of the ball. Head held back behind the ball and slightly angled so that a millisecond later by following the flight of the shot he will indeed see the underside of the ball. Give this one a try but do not overdo it.

Seek expert advice

There is a much cherished notion among golfers that once you have mastered a technique, say hitting the long irons, then you have got it for life; you will never again have any problems with long irons. Alas, golf is not like that. Even the greatest players have to make minor adjustments every time they play. Small faults or bad habits creep into the swing. Besides, nobody has ever perfected the golf swing; there is always room for further refinement.

Here we have a common sight on the European Tour, Sam Torrance

hitting shots under the critical eye of his father, Bob Torrance, an internationally respected analyst and teacher. The problem with minor faults is that the player himself is often unable to detect them; all he knows is that something is slightly wrong. The answer is to have your professional give your swing a regular check, not necessarily a full lesson but a quick once-over. A small fault, like playing with the ball slightly out of position at the address, can deteriorate, unless corrected, into a serious crisis.

Think six, play five

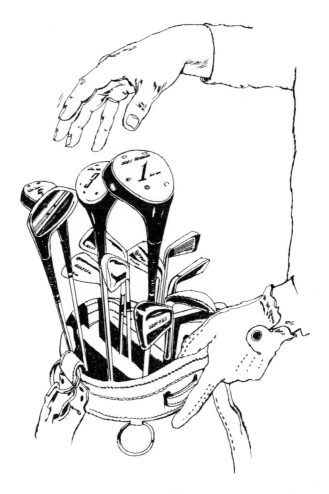

The bane of club golf is underclubbing. Taking too little club, and then either coming up short or over-hitting and hooking wide of the target, spoils more cards and loses more matches than any other fault. There may be a macho satisfaction in getting home with a blistering seven-iron at the limit of your strength but nine times out of ten those Sunday Specials come to grief.

Try this experiment. The next time you play, assess each shot and then take one more club than the one you think suitable. You may reply that you will overshoot every green but that will not happen. You will subconsciously swing more easily and the shot will be all the better for it.

Watch the worm, not the bird

The one thing every golfer knows is that the head must be kept still. If someone hits a bad shot his companions chorus: 'You lifted your head.' Sometimes they are right, because looking up prematurely to watch the result of a shot is a certain way of ensuring that the shot is not worth watching. But there are dangers in becoming obsessive about keeping the head still. It can induce rigidity in what should be a free-flowing movement. You don't think about keeping your head still when you swat a fly or hoe the carrots but you do focus intently on the object, and that it is a much better concept for golf.

A valuable exercise on every shot including putts is to develop an intense curiosity about what the ground looks like underneath the ball. Satisfy your curiosity before you look up, in the manner of today's demonstrator, Mark James. If you must follow the shot every inch of the way, visualize it in your mind's eye when you select your club and then rely on your innate talent to reproduce that glorious parabola.

Two-way stretch

Why has our artist drawn Gary Player the wrong way round? The answer is he hasn't. This is part of Player's warm-up routine on the practice ground, a sequence of full swings followed by a reversal of hands on the club for an equal number of left-handed swings. Perhaps the only other golfer to have practised as long and hard as Player was Henry Cotton and he too advocated what he called contra exercises, balancing every action with the same movements in the opposite direction.

The purpose of contra exercises, obviously enough, is to tone up the muscles of both sides of the body and prevent the development of the common lopsided posture of the golf addict. That is not a problem for the average weekend player but he too will benefit greatly from a regular exercise routine before the round because stiff muscles and creaking joints, especially after a long car drive, are an invitation to injury.

Get into the swing

It cannot be stressed too often that the action of the golf swing is simple, the simpler the better. The complications mainly arise from the golfer's mind in the form of fear – fear of a bunker, fear of making a fool of yourself, fear of topping the shot, fear of missing the green, fear of losing the match and so on. Fear comes in many guises and forms but they all have the effect of inducing tension. The muscles tighten involuntarily, rendering the player incapable of making an effective swing. The ideal is to stay completely loose throughout the swing like Mark Mouland here, as relaxed as a rag doll at the finish of a long iron shot.

It sounds like a contradiction in terms to advocate looseness if the tightening of the muscles happens involuntarily, but there is a way of fooling the nervous system with a trick. You are aware of your apprehension and the way to foil its natural consequences is to anticipate them. When you address the ball, deliberately tighten every muscle in your body as hard as you can. Strangle the club with your hands. Now relax. Let the tension flow from your body. And now make a slow, rhythmic swing.

Basic courtesy, better golf

One of the common aggravations of golf is to hit the ball flush and then, when you ask your partner or opponent: 'Where did that go?' to receive the reply: 'Sorry, but I wasn't looking.' This experience is probably at the root of that destructive fault of head-up looking to watch the flight of the ball before you have hit it. It is a basic courtesy of golf to observe all shots closely, from both friend and foe, and to mark the spot if a stray finds trouble.

If we could all rely on that simple courtesy it would be much easier to remedy the fault of prematurely raising the head. We would be free to emulate the excellent example of Ian Woosnam, here focusing on the site of the departed ball long after it has soared down the fairway. Woosnam is short, uses an abbreviated backswing and his action is markedly languid, yet he is one of the longest hitters on the Tour. His secret is timing and making a precise contact, both benefits which flow from keeping his eye on the ball.

Clear the junk from your attic

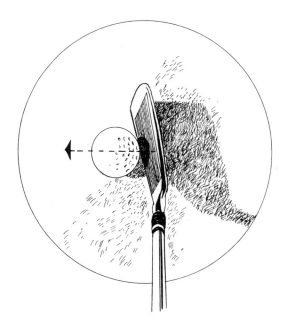

Golfers are particularly susceptible to hang-ups. I can't get on with my driver. I hate bunkers. I've never been able to hit fairway woods. The commonest neurosis is probably the fear of straight-faced clubs. Very often when you inspect a set of second-hand irons you will find that the two- and three-irons are virtually as new. You can be sure that when the owner did try to use those clubs he opened the face and tried to scoop the ball into the air, a recipe for certain disaster. It is fruitless simply to give instructions on correct technique in these cases because the fault is in the mind. That is where a remedy must be applied.

If you have no confidence in the straight-faced irons you can use psychological trickery on yourself. Address the ball in the usual way, with the blade square. Now, without adjusting your grip, rotate the hands slightly in an anticlockwise direction, thus hooding the club face. It will now look quite impossible to get the ball airborne, but have faith; that is the very message you want to implant in your subconscious. Make your usual swing, concentrating only on delivering a descending blow. Without any volition on your part your hands will square the club face at impact and, hey presto! The ball will soar into the air. As your fear dissipates, so in time you will be able to play the straight-faced irons without hooding the club at the address.

Try it backwards

Some tournament professionals have a little trick to get their swings back into the groove. Knowing what the position should be at impact, they address the ball in this posture and then swing back from there. The idea, of course, is that this recent reinforcement of muscle memory will return them to the correct impact position. For us lesser mortals this procedure suggests a valuable warm-up routine for the practice ground.

Take this study of Lee Trevino, frozen just as his swing enters the hitting zone. Address the ball normally and then, having established a proper ball position, take up this static pose, hands just below waist height, hips turned away, weight on the left foot, right elbow tucked into the body, back of the left hand facing the sky. Relax any muscular tension and complete

the swing through to a high finish. Starting from this position you should hit a crisp pitch shot.

On the next shot introduce an element of backswing, just a foot or so of hand movement as you rotate the shoulders and ease a little weight onto the right foot. This will give you a fuller shot without any conscious increase of effort. Progressively lengthen the backswing until you are completing a full swing, making sure to get your weight more and more across to the right as your backlift becomes higher and higher.

Alternate these full shots with normal swings and you are sure to acquire an effective swing pattern. No jabbing with the arms, mind. Every shot, no matter how short, must be a segment of the proper swing.

Play the percentages

It is a common fallacy that pros never share the amateur's indecision over the choice of club because their yardage charts tell them to within a yard what distance they must hit. In fact, those yardage charts constantly raise this dilemma because the pro finds himself midway between clubs, plus or minus seven or eight yards from the natural range of a club. So he has to nail his seven-iron or hit a smooth six-iron. How does he choose between them? The rule is that if you put extra beef into a shot there will be a tendency to hook, while an easy swing will tend to fade. So the selection is made by assessing which side of the target poses the greater danger.

Here we have a picture of the eighth hole of Wentworth's West course. Your ball is lying well even though just off the fairway and you judge the distance to be between clubs. You have water short of the green and to the left so the answer must be to take the longer of the two possible clubs and swing easily. That choice will give you confidence in making the distance and if you should put some fade onto the ball it will drift away from the danger, still leaving you with a possible putt for a birdie.

Nail that tack

Examine the faces of Roberto de Vicenzo's club and you will observe a spot about the size of a penny worn almost smooth from precise contact in his daily regime of hitting 400 shots. Such accuracy is the result of innate talent and a lifetime of devotion to golf, and the reward for the affable Argentinian is the largest tally of tournament victories in the history of golf.

Exact contact on every shot represents a perfection beyond the scope of weekend golfers, who must live with a proportion of slight mis-hits. There is, however, a well-tried method of improving your ratio of contacts right on the button. Instead of just looking at the ball, narrow your focus to the precise point on

the ball where you wish to make contact. Now imagine that there is a tack sticking into the ball at this point, in line with the shot but sloping slightly downwards. You have now refined your task from a broad intention to hit the ball to the more precise object of driving that imaginary tack into the ball.

If there is a secret to golf it is this meticulous defining of the objective. Inform your subconscious of your precise objective, whether it is driving to an individual daisy 220 yards up the fairway or hammering a tiny tack into the ball, and the clearer the instructions are, the more accurate the execution will be. Nebulous intentions breed nebulous results.

Don't kick yourself

The Italian World Cup player Baldovino Dassu is an immensely gifted golfer capable of extraordinary virtuosity, as when he scored 60 in the Swiss Open. His problem is that he is a perfectionist who gives himself a terribly hard time if the shape of his shot is not exactly the way he had planned it, or if the line is not precisely on the flag.

Calling yourself an idiot is a destructive process and, if you do so out loud, inconsiderate of your playing companions (who already have their opinions of you). Ben Hogan, who came closer than anyone to golfing perfection, reckoned that at best he hit no more than five strokes a round that completely satisfied him. Every golfer can scale that success rate to his level of performance, which means that a 24-handicapper can expect to hit fifty-five more or less unsatisfying shots a round, not counting putts.

There is an old saying in golf that you have to play with what you've got, and that means accepting that dream rounds belong in dreams. Plan your way around the course on the basis of your average shots, not your Sunday Specials. Shrug off those slight mis-hits and immediately begin to anticipate the most important shot in golf, the next one. If you recognize your limitations you will enjoy your golf the better and, oddly enough, you will improve.

Opening up for more distance

Open champion Sandy Lyle is particularly noted for the seemingly effortless way he hits the ball huge distances. The secret lies in the way he takes the club back. Look at that club-head. Although his shoulders have barely started to turn he has rotated his hands in a clockwise direction so the club-face is in a markedly 'open' position.

With some people this happens quite naturally and they never have to give a thought to it. Others, like Nick Faldo, have to work to acquire this move and consign it to their subconscious. The pros call this action 'fanning the blade' and it is the reverse action on the downswing, rolling the hands to bring the club-face square at impact, that gives Lyle's shots the extra zip.

Swish for length

Powerful men are often mystified and embarrassed when they are outdriven by a slightly-built girl who is clearly not even exerting herself. The reason is that length is not a product of muscular strength but club-head *speed*, which is the result of a well-timed swing. Most golfers play with a mixture of swing and hit but more often than not the hit component is the ruination of the shot, both for distance and direction. No matter how much physical effort you apply you cannot move the club-head faster than you can swing the club, and a pure swing is a relatively effortless action.

Nobody ever swung the club better than Sam Snead, whose action is devoid of effort and tension, like a man swishing the head off a daisy with his walking stick. Imagine the shaft is made of string in order to develop the feeling of a pure swing.

Swinging to work

Can you guess what this man does for a living? Note the flying right elbow, club cocked at an eccentric angle and the weight being planted solidly on the wrong foot in what the professionals call a reverse pivot. From his ruddy complexion and obvious strength, he must be a manual worker whose work keeps him toiling in the sun. You might further assume that he likes to hit balls on the driving range to release his frustrations, although you might have rather more difficulty in thinking that he could get much enjoyment playing on the course, not with that swing.

In fact this is Miller Barber, still winning tournaments on the American Senior Tour after a long and successful career on the regular American PGA Tour. His swing is highly personal, highly idiosyncratic. How does he do it? The answer is that the ball cannot see him doing everything all wrong. All the ball knows is that when the club-head makes violent contact it is doing everything right.

There is a valuable lesson to be drawn from the admirable Mr Barber: a good swing is one that works. Some people are incapable of reproducing a classical swing, perhaps for reasons of girth or infirmity, but that does not mean that they are incapable of playing classical golf. Do not be hidebound by theory; experiment and find a method that works for you.

Don't waste your strength

Our illustrations are inspired by pictures in a splendid history of Seaford Golf Club, published to celebrate the club's centenary, and by putting these two studies side by side the editor has deftly provided a graphic golf lesson for those of analytical bent.

Both players have clearly not spared themselves in their efforts to inflict grievous bodily harm on the ball. On the left Dr C. B. Gervis leans into the shot with considerable lateral movement of the upper body towards the target. This was a popular style in the days when golfers wore jackets and, while modern instructors might wince, we could label this swing 'A Fault in the Right Direction'. F. E. Lander, on the right, has put just as much effort into his drive but we can deduce that he kept his weight solidly planted on his left foot during the backswing. The action of the downswing produced the inescapable reaction, throwing his weight onto the right foot and thereby dissipating his power. 'Effort Misapplied.'

Flourish in the finish

Fifty years ago the purists would have pursed their lips at this action and crossed this candidate off the list of possibles for an international cap. The classic style then was to hit against a braced left leg. Paul Way has not done too badly in the Walker Cup, Ryder Cup and PGA championship with his knee-slide, reminiscent of Tom Watson in the early days. This is not necessarily a style to be copied but it perfectly illustrates the fundamental virtue of an effective swing.

The swing path is like a wheel rotating on an inclined axle and it can only work if the axle is held firmly. The feet anchor one end of the axle but the other end, located at the back of the lower neck, is free to wobble about if we permit it to do so. Way's axle is firm, allowing the rest of him to spin freely to a flowing, uninhibited finish.

Aim the gun

The Japanese professional Koichi Uehara has an unorthodox backlift of the club, as eccentric as the actions of Gay Brewer, Eamon Darcy or Miller Barber. Personal foibles in the swing – and even the great Bobby Jones had a pronounced looping action – are permissible provided that the club settles into the path of righteousness in time for the business part of the swing. When he gets to here, approaching the top of the backswing, Uehara is a model of orthodoxy.

The next time you pass a full-length mirror, or catch your reflection in the club-house window, swing back to this position and check whether your club, like his, is pointing like a gun barrel directly at the ball. If not, then either the ball or your swing plane is out of position.

Setting the angle

Here, you might think, is a rank novice down at the driving range and trying his hand at golf for the first time. He has no idea, cocking his wrists before he starts his upswing and taking the club-head back along quite the wrong line. He'll be lucky if he hits the ball at all.

But wait. This Corey Pavin, ranked among the ten best players in the world; he must be doing something right. In fact he is doing everything right and what makes his swing look so peculiar is that he has his own sequence for doing the right things.

Starting the upswing by rolling the wrists to an open position might help your game. After all, Nancy Lopez, who is among the ten best women golfers in the world, does much the same thing. The pros call this 'setting the angle early' and from here all you do is make a full turn, arriving at the top in an orthodox position. Pavin swings very flat and gives the ball a big lash with the hands but he doesn't half give it a clout and he is uncommonly straight with it. You can see from his follow-through that he has not spared himself.

When wrong becomes right

As with the killing of cats, there are more ways than one of playing golf and here we illustrate two extremes, with particular emphasis on the position of the right elbow. Purists would call these bad positions but most of use would settle for playing as well as George Burns or Bobby Clampett, either with the flying right elbow, almost vertical swing and shut-faced action of Burns or with Clampett's flat swing, open face and right elbow superglued to his side. So should these styles be copied, and if so which?

The answer must be no in both cases but there is a lesson to be learned: deviations from orthodoxy are permissible *provided that the golfer compensates for them by the time the club-head reaches the ball.* The critical factors in hitting the ball are that the club-head must contact the ball along the correct angle of attack, on the line of the shot, with the centre of the club-face making contact, with the club-face square to the target line and at speed. It does not really matter how you achieve those five objectives and if personal idiosyncracies of swing help you meet those objectives consistently then that is fine; it is just that it is easier for most people to succeed with an orthodox method.

Faulty powers

Here is one for you golf purists. How many faults can you detect in the set-up of this player?

Would you say that he is favouring his weight on the left foot? Certainly.

What about that left-hand grip? Isn't it too far on top of the shaft? Absolutely.

And are his hands much too far ahead of the ball? Right again.

The headgear! Surely that is more suitable for a lady lawn-tennis player? Bang on, we can all agree on that one.

So what lesson can we seekers after golf truth draw from this illustration in order to lower our scores in the monthly medal? Make wholesale corrections to grip and address position? No. The lesson is that if you hit the ball as well as the hugely gifted Philip Parkin, then leave well alone. Minor deviations from theoretical perfection are permissible provided that the swing works.

Slow and short to keep in swing

It seems logical to suppose that if you want to hit the ball longer you should swing the club back farther. That is true of half shots and three-quarter shots with a pitching club, but for full shots logic gives way to paradox. The trick of hitting the ball a long way is not to make a fuller swing or a more violent swing but to make more precise contact with the ball, to hit it right on the button. And the way to achieve this precision may well be to shorten the swing and slow everything down.

Ronan Rafferty, who gives the ball a fierce wallop, believes that it is unnecessary ever to raise the hands above shoulder height, give or take an inch or so. He is immensely strong, of course, but it remains true that it is easier to maintain control of the club-head with an economical backswing. Experiment with this idea if you are having problems making solid contact with the ball.

Genuflect in respect to age

Peter Butler has one of the simplest and most enduring swings in British golf and if you are one of those unfortunates who suffer from the topped shot, failing to get the blade of the club to the bottom of the ball, then you might take a leaf out of Butler's book. He makes a slight but distinct dip with the knees as he comes in to the ball, making sure that he delivers a descending blow down and through the ball.

This bobbing action is often of particular benefit for the portly and the elderly whose bodies are not as supple as of yore. Before adopting the Butler bob, it is worth checking that your tendency to top and ball is not caused by flapping at the ball with hands and arms instead of generating club-head speed through rotation of the shoulders. The club is swung by spinning the upper body and the function of the arms is mainly to connect that power source to the golf club.

Brace for balance

Gene Littler has the swing which the other pros would like to steal and the particular virtue which we might examine in this study is balance, the absolute foundation of good golf. It is true enough that if the path of the club-head is orthodox and the upswing slow enough, leg action will take care of itself without any conscious thought. But, alas, we do not all have orthodox swings and some of us, indeed most of us, swing too fast. What can happen is that during the upswing, as the weight is naturally transferred onto the right foot, the weight goes too far to the right, buckling the right ankle. Balance is lost and along with it any possibility of making an effective swing.

Notice how Littler's braced right leg keeps his weight concentrated on the inside of his right foot. If you have this problem of swaying off balance on the backswing, put in a good session on the practice ground and hit every shot with a golf ball tucked under the sole of your right shoe, just below the root of the little toe. That should cure your sway, especially if you slow down the backswing.

Rehearse the performance

Most people start to play golf by gripping the club, and then swinging it, in the way which instinct suggests is the most effective. That instinct is a tyrannical slave-master whose domination is fiendishly difficult to defy. The pro gives a lesson to a pupil who begins to hit the ball quite well on the practice ground but when he gets onto the course in the heat of battle he reverts to the commands of instinct. The longer you play the harder it becomes to break the shackles of instinct.

After a dozen years of virtually daily golf Nick Faldo determined to reshape his swing. He spent two years reprogramming his instincts and still he had to remind himself before each shot of the key to his new action, hence this distinctive waggle. Faldo's key is to roll the club-face open, what the pros call setting the angle, and it might work for you. But the real lesson is that if you are incorporating an improvement into your swing, as the result of expert advice, of course, be sure to rehearse it before every swing as a last-minute reminder.